Up
Your
Value

How to really grow your business

by
Dennis O'Neill
the business growth coach

Up Your Value

How to really grow your business

ISBN: 0-7596-7546-5

This book is printed on acid free paper.

1stBooks – rev. 02/28/02

What's in it for you...(index)

v

introduction

Why this book?

"**Value** is the key word of the new millenium"suggests my long-time friend Mel Cooper, owner of Seacoast Communications of Victoria BC

Marketing strategy is 'how you deliver <u>value</u>' says Peter Drucker. More than ever, marketing concerns itself with delivering value.

Now more than ever *the value questions* stand out front and center.

The VALUE questions

What is value?

How do customers evaluate?

How do you go about delivering value?

What are the most effective value strategies?

Which value tactics prove most efficient and competitive?

How do you develop the most profitable value-marketing system?

How do "value" and your internal "values" connect?

My VALUE MISSION

The only way anyone can increase revenue
is to increase value for someone else.

So, what mission motivates Dennis O'Neill,
the business coach? What is it that I do?

I *'UP YOUR VALUE'* (in 3 ways):

1. help you become more valuable personally
   …as a person, manager, marketer,
2. help make your product/service more
   valuable
3. help make your company more valuable…
   (increasing value of the corporate assets)

Desired outcome for you

This book boosts you as…………

a VALUE EXPERT.

Appreciation

I've been told I was born on third base since I was blessed with two exceptionally wonderful parents who never stopped doing things for me. I still have my Dad, James Gordon O'Neill who at age 92 is in the process of publishing his memoirs *"OF OTHER DAYS AROUND ME"* and also a book of poetry entitled *"FURROWS OF FANCY*. Dad you inspire me every single day.

I thank my wife Margaret for her support over 28 years and for her patience during the book writing. Her technology breakthru's for me really salvaged the project. (I am at times software challenged)

To the Sage of Allanburg, I offer my deep appreciation for your wisdom and mentoring. Few people have the advantage of 'learning at the feet of Socrates' as I have been privileged to do.

Thank you to my clients who are also my friends. You make my career an exciting and rewarding adventure.

What ENGINES drive your business?

% of your total revenue derived from each engine

[%] direct sales force
[%] repeat business / loyalty plan
[%] sustained advertising

[%] promotional systems
[%] direct marketing / database
[%] telemarketing

[%] e-commerce
[%] location / landmark, drive-by, walk-by, sign
[%] reputation / pro-active word of mouth

[%] referrals
[%] lead generating system. e.g. networking
[%] sales development program
          (new products/services)
[%] cross promotion partners
[%] barter
[%] what else?_____

100% total

Do you need more engines, or do they need more fuel?
Dennis O'Neill   the business growth coach

Chapter 1
Mission Impossible!

For sure, because they forgot *"the mission statement"*.

How do you feel about boarding an airplane with no definite flight plan which says... "destination ...SOMEWHERE, Departure and arrival times...WHENEVER... route... WHATEVER."

What you really wanted was to fly today's 5 p.m. American Airlines flight 658- arriving New York's Kennedy Airport at 6:05 p.m.

So many businesses "file no definite flight plan", no mission statement. Why? They've seen one of those run-on "mission statements" cluttering somebody's reception area. Well-meaning maybe, but with 9 dangling participles, and run-on sentences it's more of a maze than a mission.

The "effective" MISSION STATEMENT has three words.

Make that three! - 3 words -. Bill Clinton became President with a 3-worder..."**The economy stupid**". No matter what, Mr. Clinton routed discussion back to THE election issue...the economy. It worked.

The memory factor
How clear it gets when every employee in an organization knows what we are all trying to do.(in 3 words). They can remember 3 words.

Fedex
Fedex has it down. **"GET IT THERE"**. That's it. Excuses don't count. When I take them a package, what do I want? "Get it there". Test them and see! I did. I had a package that a client of mine said he had to have by 2 o'clock the next day. The Fedex employee said "We wouldn't normally deliver there until 5 o'clock." She picked up the phone and said "How can we get this package to Toronto by 2 p.m. tomorrow?" She didn't say "Can we get it there, but How can we?" You see the difference in attitude. That's what a clear mission statement does.

I'm positioned as "The Business Growth Coach". So, what's my 3 word mission statement?...

"**Up your value!**" Simple…because that's all I do.

My client, the Victorian Inn in Stratford Ontario now operates with the mission…

"BRING GUESTS BACK". Does it work? "Since we put in the 3-word mission statement, 90% of our staff are working at a higher level" says Dyan Drummond, part owner.

The Artful Cookie franchise chain faced the mission question. The first issue was to determine what business they are in. And it's not the "cookie business". The delivery may be bouquets of "longstem" cookies wrapped in colorful cellophane…but, the end product is the joyful smile of the person receiving the cookie bouquet. What is the mission statement? **"MAKE SOMEONE SMILE".** It's the mission for the person pleasantly taking the order, the person correctly putting together the specifications, the person proudly delivering the bouquet. Indeed everybody!

Brian Knot, Brantford Ontario's Golf Doctor has it right. His coaching instruction, video taping, made-to-order clubs, golf equipment and clothing etc…all are focused by his mission statement…"**PLAY BETTER GOLF**".

When Tom Monaghan had just one Dominos Pizza location, he crystallized his mission...**PIZZA FAST, PIZZA HOT**. He built his team on that clear mission. Then he guaranteed the public..."Delivered in 30 minutes or the pizza is free."

Pepsi Cola's mission?- **"BEAT COKE"**.

Rich's Dairy?— **"WORLD CLASS"**.

Don't think of your Mission Statement as just some academic exercise. Make it an agent of focus. Watch your organization get clear! Want to see your organization harnessed together in unity? **What's your mission statement—in 3 words or less?**

Clear mission adds value.

Chapter 2
The value of your VISION

How clear is the **business vision** that drives your enterprise? Who can succeed in business without a dream…a VISION of the successful end?…the lure and beacon to draw and guide the entrepreneur.

The business vision is your reason, your inspiration, your driving force, your ever-recharging energy supply, your direction.

* How clear is your vision and **vision statement**?
* How well do you paint your vision to financial backers? To employees? To customers? To suppliers?
* Does the vision have value? What's it worth? Doesn't everyone connected with your organization want to know where you are going?

Have you watched a business when the operators lack a vision? Indecision. Uncertainty.

Disagreement. Futility. Without that vision, watch a business get choked out fast.

VISION versus MISSION

What's the difference?

The **vision** statement *shows* destination (**where**).

The **mission** *statement **tells*** the means (**how**).

Vision statement says where we want to go. Mission tells us how we get there.

I like to keep it short and concise.

The Artful Cookie franchise chain sells cookie bouquets. Their vision is "*a franchise in every Ontario city*".(where they want to get to). Their mission statement is "*Make Someone Smile*". This mission is the service means by which they will do it. The mission of every person at The Artful Cookie is to "Make Someone Smile".

Let's consider the value of your vision statement. Suppose you are franchising your business. If your vision is to have franchises all over, what does that do to a single potential franchisee? If I want to buy one of your franchises, isn't it worth a lot to me knowing that the vision offers one in every city. People everywhere will become aware of the business. People moving to my city will already know of my business name and services. People from my city will visit other cities and see franchises in those cities. They will come back more aware of the name, the service, and our success record elsewhere.

Your vision statement provides an opportunity to create value.

When I think about vision statements, I think of Alice in Wonderland...

ALICE..."Would you tell me please, which way I ought to go from here?"

MAD HATTER..."That depends a good deal on where you want to get to."

ALICE..."Well, I don't really much care."

MAD HATTER..."Then it doesn't matter which way you go."

Leaders can gain followers by crystallizing a vision. It's *where we want to go*! Vision helps others see "what's in it for me". And, wouldn't it be jolly nice businesswise, if we (our whole team) are all traveling to the same destination, the same vision.

examples...Land's End—Become the world's largest seller clothing

Starbucks—Be the largest coffee seller in the world. Mine is— Be recognized as the Value guru

So, where are you going? **WHAT IS YOUR VISION STATEMENT?**

Chapter 3
Reframing Change as value opportunity

Do we see change as opportunity?

Change. Some see it as bad. Some see it as good. Others are oblivious to it. They just go on as always. What things are changing? Or, should we ask, what isn't changing?

Change is for sure

One thing stands certain; increasingly rapid change has overtaken us. Publisher Rupert Murdoch says "the sum total of human knowledge is doubling every 20 months." Doesn't that fact alone ensure change. It's been said that the next 10 years will bring more changes than the previous 2,000.

Out with old paradigms

Charles Exley, CEO of NCR Corp. spoke profoundly when he said ...

"I've been in this business 36 years. I've learned a lot—and most of it doesn't apply anymore."

Or, as a sign at NASA headquarters says... "If it works, it's obsolete."

Change is opportunity

Consider the good news...in times of rapid change, everybody goes back to zero. Change brings new rules. It's like beginning all over, every organization from the same starting point. If you're the little guy, that doesn't sound so awful.

Who can escape change? Is change disruptive? Is change all bad?

Can change act as your ally and friend? How do we handle change?

All of a sudden, are you starting to feel a little more confident? Do these possibilities cross your mind "Maybe I'm not as far behind as I thought in this competitive world"? "Maybe change has hit others harder than me." Or, "maybe I've even got an edge on the competition."

How to Handle Change

1. **KNOW THE TRENDS** If you tune to the trends you're ahead of most people.

2. **DO YOUR HOMEWORK** Marketers have to function as FULL-TIME STUDENTS OF CHANGE.

3. **SCRUB OUT OLD PARADIGMS** "To make significant changes, people need to change how they solve problems and how they view the world—they need to make a paradigm shift." quote from Harvey Gelman

4. **BE SERIOUS ABOUT IT** "If you always do what you always did, you will always get what you always got." Change. Adapt. Adjust. Modify. Reconfigure. Alter. Exchange. Renew. Transform.

"Those who master change succeed. Those who don't fail."

How well do you seize the opportunities of change?

Chapter 4
Value on purpose. GOALS

He shoots. He scores. NOT Imagine Stanley Cup hockey with NO GOALS. The 2 teams are on the ice…but there are no nets.

How will we know who wins?

That's the way most people play the game of life. Without goals. Having no clearly defined written objectives. Does your business have specific written goals for the year? Are you planning to fail? No written goals means just that.

PURPOSE

Have you personal long-term, medium term and short term goals? The quickest way to identify your long-term goal is to ask yourself what you want written on your epitaph. That long-term goal is like a north pole attracting your everyday compass.

Still having trouble? Read *"THE POWER OF PURPOSE"* by Richard J Leider.

Someone defined a goal as "a dream set within a time-frame." That dream acts like a beacon, attracting us, ever-drawing on us.

Goal-setting gets talked about, but who does it? "In the absence of clearly defined goals, we are forced to concentrate on activity, and ultimately become enslaved by it." Lots of people look busy as they go nowhere. It's Parkinson's Law.

SMART GOALS

Specific	clearly defined, written down
Measurable	'a goal without a number is just a slogan' says The Sage of Allanburg
Aspiring	pushing your reach a little
Realistic	practical and achievable, accompanied by a plan
Timely	having a time frame to prod you to get done

TODAY GOALS

As a friend of mine asks..."Did you have a good day? How would you know?" Ask...What am I doing TODAY to make each of my goals for the year happen?

Clear goals make it possible to advance every step with effectiveness & efficiency.

Once written, put your goals out so they can hit you in the face. My March weight loss goal on my wall shouted "Get to 167 pounds by August 31." Done.

You might want to share goals with a friend who will encourage you along the way. Don't forget to reward yourself for achieving milestones.

"Obstacles are those frightful things you see when you fail to focus on your goals."

Have you found out how much you really can achieve?

Make it a goal. Then set out the planned steps to achieve the goal.

Chapter 5
Show me your business MAP

Identify Your
<u>M</u>ain <u>A</u>ction <u>P</u>riorities-
Your "**MAP**" to Value.

Ever notice that most good cooks work with a recipe? So do good marketers. Keep the hoping and guessing to a minimum.

Every year every business absolutely must produce **a one-page written marketing plan— your ROADMAP** showing how to get from here to where you want to be in a year.

MAP versus a "Business Plan"

Keep the Marketing Plan Simple! You don't need to present a thick book. Maybe your financial backers or the bank require the longer type called a "business plan". It forces you to explore all the issues in start-up. "The business plan" generally gets filed on a backroom shelf and never sees the light of day again. It served its purpose... making you think things through.

The MAP is one page. Keep it in your wallet if you like, or on the wall. Mine is beside my computer.

Revisions

If major market upheavals take place, tear up your one-pager MAP and do a new one that reflects the changed conditions. That's O.K. It's not chiseled in stone.

Budget

The Roadmap/marketing plan should be accompanied by a budget to make it happen. Having a one page operating plan(MAP) makes the process simple.

Easy MAP Preparation

Don't complicate it. The simplest way is to make a grid with 5 vertical columns and 5 or 6 lined horrizontal.

Down the left-hand vertical **column A**, identify (hopefully in a single word each), your 5 or 6 Main Action Priorities, or MAP's... (the main issues you must confront)...the things that if achieved, will make this a successful year. For example your MAP's might be...

Sales, Expenses, Marketing, Training, New location, Suppliers

After you have isolated your Main Action Priorities, and have completed the vertical columns, you will need to revisit them and arrange them in Priority. You may want to number them from 1 to 5 or 6.

In **Column B**, (beside each of the single word MAP's from column A), define in as few words as possible, your specific objective. It's possible that you may have more than one specific objective for an individual MAP item.

In **Column C** list specific actions (your action plan) to help achieve each specific objective. There may be one action or 2, or maybe even 10 actions or more for a specific objective. Column C may need to be wider than the other columns.

Review the list and ask yourself...If I complete all of these actions, will I have achieved my objective? If not, you need to add other actions until you hold strong confidence that these actions will achieve the objective.

In **Column D** indicate the manner in which you will measure success in that goal. This factor proves toughest for most people. We really operate with impoverished thinking in how to measure our actions. Spend time finding the ways to measure. More on measurement later.

In **Column E** give a time frame of when you will review progress for that aspect. It's too late to prod yourself if you wait to year-end and have not made sufficient progress. The review is the prod. Use it as an early warning system. You will probably want to have another person involved in the review of one or more lines if they have involvement.

The page looks like this:

Business MAP (Main Action Priorities)

A 5 MAP's	B Objective	C Action Plan	D Measurement	E Review
1				
2				
3				
4				
5				

Business MAP payoffs

Having the "MAP" written out allows you to study it and perhaps polish certain items. Once you have your "MAP" fine-tuned, you can share it with a spouse, shareholders, with any employees, part-time employees, etc. They can quickly see where you plan to go and how you will get there. They can see your agenda. They can raise any weak spots that might need bolstering and polish it. Now other team members can fully support you.

<u>MAPs *STAGE TWO*</u>

Once you have your MAP (***Main Action Priorities***) completed and installed,

1. Have you shown it to your key people?

Would those key people benefit from knowing what are your most important objectives?... so that they can support you?

Would it benefit you to ensure the entire team is pulling in the same direction, not everybody's own direction?

2. Would it now be effective to ask your key people to fill out a MAP sheet of their own?

Would you benefit from knowing what they are working towards? Would they achieve more by having their objectives committed to paper and committed to mentally?

Now you can reap the benefits gained from having **the whole team harnessed together in unity** *and* **pulling the same direction.**

Chapter 6
Value patterns

Model after winners!
Take the best from each.

Who are your models of excellence? Which 5 companies rate best in your field? What does each do better than anyone else? Can you pattern after them?

Ask a salesperson in most industries "which 5 sales people in your industry rank at the top?" The usual answer... "I don't know." Sales people have no corner on the market here; most business people wouldn't know. Seldom have they ever thought of who might be the 5 best models in their field, or even the single best.

Ah, but ...ask an athlete. Who are the 5 best in their sport and they'll come right back with the top 5 in order. References. Models. Patterns. Outstanding examples. In sports they have models of excellence to rise to. Don't Olympic competitors keep a book on competitors? times, weights, training schedules, etc.

Businesses can and must upgrade, improve, grow, shine. How can they if they've never taken note of those businesses who excel in the specific areas they compete in? Who and what do we have to beat?

In customer service, what are the 5 best examples you can think of? What can you and I do to emulate their feats? What does each one do that makes them better?

In sales who are the 5 absolute best people in your field? What does each do to make them the best? Would any of those people be willing to offer advice?

Advertising has its outstanding practitioners. What do the 5 best advertisers in your field do?

What 5 companies in any field execute the best overall marketing thrust? I've chosen my 5 and keep a file on each. They teach me some spectacular lessons.

What way teaches us best?...watching poor examples and mistakes, or watching great examples..the best examples?

As Yogi says...."You can observe a lot just by looking."

Business growth turns up a whole lot easier when we pattern ourselves after the ideal, not after the poor and idle.

Dennis O'Neill

Who can you find as your best pattern to model after, your patterns of excellence?

Chapter 7
The value formula

No VALUE—No Sale!

What is Value in marketing all about?

Victor Kiam owned the Remington Shaver Company. You know, "he liked it so much he bought the company." Well he also had the chance to buy Velcro. But he didn't. Why? *He didn't see the value.* **The reason people don't buy something, or anything is …THEY DON'T SEE THE VALUE.**

What is value? How do people ***evaluate***? What simple formula will guide marketers in delivering value? Consider the value formula I use to truly simplify the whole marketing process.

VALUE = $\frac{\text{Need} + \text{Trust}}{\text{Price}}$

How simple! Whether people know it or not, they **subconsciously evaluate by this formula.**

NEED

If I have no need for something, it has no value to me. The more I need something, the more value it has to me and the more I am willing to pay for it. Something may have value to one person and not to another person. It depends on need.

In the beginning McDonald's created a multi-billion dollar company based on executing this formula, whether they were aware of using the formula or not. They did not come out saying they have the world's greatest hamburger. They built their growth on "You deserve a break today."

They spoke to the need…a break…for folks all over America. Mom needed a break from the dishes and from meal preparation. They hit the need. McDonald's pointed out that need to Moms, Dads, and Kids. We didn't need a hamburger; but my wife and I needed a break. A hamburger managed to fill the need inexpensively and conveniently.   So America buys billions of hamburgers to fill the need for a break.

TRUST

Even when I have a great need for something, I won't necessarily buy a specific product. Let's say in the middle of winter, you come down with a terrible cough. I am a complete stranger to you and say... "I have just the thing for you here in this bottle". It's a clear glass bottle with no label, and no markings. The liquid is a brownish green that could be swamp water or worse. You don't know me. There's no name. Do you trust this product? I don't think so. You may have need but without *trust* it doesn't rate. You'll probably pass on this product.

McDonald's built trust with their systems that always delivered the same product and service whether it was in St. Catharines, Ontario or Little Rock, Arkansas. They were always clean and you could spot them from a distance by the golden arches. Trust. You could count on them and they always had something for the kids. They really deserve credit for giving us a trustworthy national standard in clean bathrooms. Where did you go before McDonalds when you had to travel? It was scary.   It takes NEED plus TRUST to deliver value. Need on the part of the customer. Trust in the seller/manufacturer/product.

PRICE

Any price is too much if I don't need something. The greater the need, the more one can raise the price. The more trust that is built in the product or seller, the greater the capacity to charge for it .

You can raise the price if the need increases. You can charge more when you build trust with the buyer. This formula (value = $\frac{\text{need} + \text{trust}}{\text{price}}$) forms the basis of value marketing.

Value selling

The selling system I use has this simple formula as its basis. The only way to increase revenue is to add value for someone else. How?

1) Find the **need**. Demonstrate the need. Prove the need.
2) Build **trust**. Reputation. Deliver over time. Show concern for the client. Spending time identifying their real need goes a long way. Use third party testimonials. Work on the many ways of producing trust. Make a list

of how you can build trust with your customers.

3) Ensure the need and trust factors equal or exceed the **price**.

Simple!…and it works.

Chapter 8
Values…
basis for all our decisions

Your values are your priorities-
the things most important to you.

DECISION PROCESS

All decisions and behavior are based on our values. Everything you decide hinges on your values. Values determine what your customers decide. What are their values? Values balance between "values towards", (things wanted) e.g. wealth or gain, or "values away" (things avoided) e.g. pain. I define values as "The goal posts and foul lines in the game of life".

UNDERSTANDING THE MARKETPLACE

The VALS Study in the U.S. breaks the population down into 8 different groups based on their values. AT&T sought one group.

Concentrated in the Midwest, the group's chief value is family. So AT&T used the theme "reach out and touch someone". Long distance usage with that group increased by 1000%.

Do you want to press their hot button…touch their values.

SOCIETAL VALUES

A late 80's U.S. Newspaper Advertising Bureau study revealed the then 8 major societal values:

1. self-esteem　　　　*2. warm relationships*
3. security　　　　*4. time*
5. fun/enjoyment/excitement
6. self-fulfillment　　*7. health & fitness*
8. belonging/nostalgia/localism

Societal values are continually changing. Norman Cetron offered his list of 74 trends to *FUTURIST Magazine*. He includes shifts in societal values, notably from the "me" ethic of the 80's to the 90's "family ethic". Within society individual values may vary considerably.

Personal values

I have identified and prioritized my own values, a revealing exercise. What are your personal values? If you really want to know yourself, identify your values .

VALUES-BASED SELLING

Selling psychology has long focused on stressing benefits, not features. While this is valid, the benefit must touch a customer value. Consider a new liquid detergent...

features...grease-cutting ingredient

benefits...gets dishes sparkling clean

values...homemaker's reputation sparkles

What's more important, sparkling dishes or sparkling reputation? Sure, reputation.

Buying

Buying employs basically an emotional response, based on the individual's values. From a broad assortment of values, marketing may want to touch these: *Pride of ownership. Savings and economy. Love and affection. Security and protection. Luxury and convenience.* Values seem equal till someone points out a difference.

Value is based on values… the buyer's, not the seller's.

CORPORATE VALUES

Corporate values sway behavior, recruiting, end product. Witness Disney's values:

1. Quality	*2. Learning*
3. Having Fun	*4. "Guest" concept*
5. Conservation	*6. Value perception*
7. Curiosity	*8. Family Entertainment*
9. Teamwork	*10. Patriotism*

What are your business values?

Identifying them helps understand your decisions.

IDENTIFYING VALUES

To isolate specific values in any situation, there are two questions that do it.

What's most important to you **in**…, (your marketing), (your advertising), (your purchase of…), (your life), etc. Now we know a person's values.

What specifically would you need to have happen, (to feel),…(to think),…(to experience), the values answered in question one. From this answer we determine if we are serving the persons' values.

CONCLUSION

Ben Franklin said…"In persuasion, talk of emotion (spelled VALUES) not reason".

Do you know your own personal values? Have you identified the values of your best customers?

Chapter 9
Value-Added...How?

Who doesn't want the most for their money? Customers decisions sway to the choice that offers something extra. How does a business offer more? How does a business offer more without increasing expenses or losing profitability? What does added value mean:

Increased Revenue

Increased revenue comes only one way...by adding value for the customer.

How do you add value? You must add a customer benefit. The key is to produce the benefit for low cost or no cost. It takes creativity or smarts.

Examples of value added

Birk's Jewelers add prestige to a gift by the "blue box" they package it in. That blue box says its a quality gift, not a cheap imitation. People feel special when they get a gift in a Birk's "blue box". Customers are willing to pay the price for the special prestige feeling. The actual cost of the blue box is minimal. The perceived value is major.

Ralph Lauren adds value to his line of Polo Shirts. That little horse and rider logo says this shirt's unique. It adds a sort of "snob appeal", a social status symbol.

Reward plans can be a form of added value when they offer something on which the customer places a good value. Airline points for instance. Airlines put up what in most cases is unsold inventory and use it for leverage with their customers.

Cow Brand Baking Soda adds value by suggesting an additional use…as an odor remover in the refrigerator. Most customers need that additional use and get added value. The added need/use added nothing to the price.

A dash of creativity

The name can add value. Want to buy a round plastic disc? How about a Frisbee!

Food companies can add value to their product by supplying recipes with ideas of how to use their product.

If you are in sales and you send out an informative article to a client, you add value by using a yellow highlighter to indicate the key points. That saves the other person the time of having to read unimportant passages.

Try Synergy (1 + 1 = 7)

Added value often comes through synergy. For instance, take the situation of three organizations combining to do a promotion. A media company has unsold advertising time or space, a hotel has an empty meeting room and a marketing organization has speakers and subject material. By working together and finding a theme of solid interest they produce a seminar series that creates demand to a niche of businesses. Individually, they have unsold products and services. When combined, those products and services take on a new value for customers. The whole is greater than the sum of the parts. Added value.

Two carpenters together can achieve considerably more than two carpenters working individually. Networking with other people and organizations can often produce a team that can out-produce the efforts of the individuals if they had worked independently.

Value added can come in the form of combining or packaging. Grocers put salad dressings next to produce. Seen together, the products take on a value simply by the suggestion of their combined use in a salad.

Added Value and Pricing

Added value doesn't have to mean something for nothing, or discount. Added value means win/win. It means something the customer wants or needs and the benefit is produced by our thinking smarter. The benefit winds up being of more value than any added cost. Added value doesn't have to mean giving the benefit away. The added value factor sometimes allows you to charge more and the customer still perceives having gotten more for the money...better value.

Value in the relationship

Inc. Magazine offered a neat profound quote. "Value added is not in the product any more; it's in the relationship between the customer and sales rep."

Do you and your staff add value to the customer relationship?

Have you seriously focused enough on adding value to your product/service?

Chapter 10
Value in a new suit

Unsuspectingly a neat little marketing drama unfolded ushering in the new marketing game for me and a new client.

On a pleasant spring day a few years ago Don Ludlow offered me a warm welcome as we sat down in my first face-to-face coaching session for his business. Ludlows Menswear offers high-end mens clothing, limited shoe lines, and superb service in Brantford Ontario.

Don and I got deep in discourse about the changing marketplace, new opportunities, and particularly the effects of the Internet, websites, e-commerce and all. Don said he would be a hard sell to get into Internet marketing.

At that point Don was asked to take an important phone call only to find no one at the other end. A little strange…but we continued.

Later back at my office, a message said 'phone Don Ludlow'. He recalled our phone interruption with no one at the other end and how the person called back later. A man from England wanted a particular pair of Rockport Shoes not available over there.   The caller had searched the Internet. There he found Rockport's list of dealers from which he elected to call Don Ludlow in Brantford Ontario Canada.

As Don said, "there you were talking about all this Buck Rogers[*] stuff and a guy from England, shopping on the Internet, calls to buy Rockport shoes from me".   We both saw the irony in the timing not to mention the humor.

We had just witnessed a stage entrance of marketing's new drummer, TECHNOLOGY. Prepare for the Internet to totally defy old-style marketing with its new technologies. Also, expect more technologies than just the Internet to come swinging the sword of change to the rules of value marketing.

Value marketing is putting on its **brand new suit** with dramatic flare.

How prepared are you for CHANGE as it arrives in cascading form?

---

[*] *'Buck Rogers' a science fiction series appeared in 1929 as a comic strip, then on radio from 1932-40 and on NBC TV in the 1980's. Buck, a present-day astronaut, gets frozen while on a space mission and wakes up 500 years later in the 25th century.*

Dennis O'Neill

How well do you use the web to add value to your business?

Chapter 11
What business are you in?

What business are you really in?

"When it leaves the factory, it's lipstick, but when it crosses the counter in the department store, it's hope." (Charles Revson, former head Revlon Cosmetics.)

What business are McDonald's in? Most people say hamburgers or fast foods. But what do they say? They are in the 'systems business'. When you buy a McDonald's franchise, what are you buying? Is it several truckloads of hamburgs? Or, are you buying their well developed systems...customer service systems, promotions systems, food preparation systems etc.?

WOW

When I first met Jayna Faragher, owner of the Artful Cookie franchise chain, I asked her what business she was in. She replied "Cookies". So I said, your competition then would be Dave Nichols President's Choice chocolate chip cookies.

"Well, No", she said. I replied, He's in cookies, so what business are you in? "I don't know" said Jayna. When someone receives one of your fabulous colorful cellophane-wrapped long-stem-cookie bouquets, what do they say? She said, "They say, WOW". When they are saying wow, what is the look on their face? "A big smile", she said. So what business is she in?: The WOW business or the "*make someone smile*" business! I won't pay $18 to $35 for a dozen cookies even if they are the best, but how much will I pay to bring a smile to the face of a sick person, or someone who has just earned congratulations, or to bring birthday joy, or to make an anniversary special!

Magical store

After one of my marketing seminars, a lady asked if I would consult for her. Marilyn Bell's business card said Lyn Bell Designs. I wasn't sure then what business she was in. Perhaps floral designs, interior designs or what? Soon I found that Marilyn operates a magical ladies fashions store in an elegant Victorian house in St. George Ontario. Customers tend to be over 40, when women may begin to doubt their beauty and start to need larger sizes. Marilyn anticipates their need and does the designing herself. They're not off the rack from mass manufacturers. Customers experience a special place. Marilyn and I strived several months to capture the correct positioning. Al Ries and Jack Trout talk about "the little ladders" in peoples' heads. Each product ladder represents a product category. The product category here is women's clothing, or fashions, not design.

Voila:

Lyn Bell of St. George
FASHIONS that say you're beautiful

Look to the end result

With my own business, I faced the same question...What business am I in? I had been saying 'marketing consulting'. Two problems. One, the word marketing has different meanings to different people. Some use it to mean selling. Others use it interchangeably with advertising. The word brings confusion, not communication. Secondly, consultants exist by the army-full in all shades of specialization. That's a lot of competition from people who don't really compete at all. What is it that I do? I am a business growth coach. That's all I do. I am in the business growth business. Mission statement..."Up Your Value". My positioning liner is "The business growth coach". Do people think they need a marketing consultant? Usually not. Do they feel they can stand some "business growth"? Absolutely.

What's Ralph Lauren's business? "Manufacturers make products, I make dreams." Everytime you see what it costs for a Polo Shirt, be sure to know that Mr. Lauren knows what business he's in.

What business are you in? Are you sure? Think about it.

What business are you really in?
What's your real Value delivery?

Chapter 12
Most valued customers-20/80

The Constitution has it wrong!
In marketing…all of us are NOT equal.

Pareto's 20/80 rule says 20% of customers do 80% of sales.

My own research in Niagara Region shows 82% of Canadian border shopping trips to the U.S are done by 34% of the population.

A large food chain in my area knows that over 50% of their sales come from just 10% of their customers.

Did you know 4% of the U.S. population buy 70% of the airline trips? Do airlines treat everyone equally? A market study I did many years ago showed that 1% of Montrealers purchased 60% of the airline tickets sold to Montrealers back then. Airlines quickly learned to pamper frequent flyers.

This critical heavy-user concept changes how we advertise and promote. It affects our customer service focus. How about the need for a loyalty program! Pareto's 20/80 points to a whole new marketing strategy.

By the way, 20/80 applies to employees and products too, not just sales and customers. As a client of mine said, "You know when you lose a Pareto employee because it takes 5 people to replace them". In a retail operation, 20% of the products on the shelf will bring in 80% of the dollars.

Have you identified your most valuable 20/80 customers? If you don't know how, get help fast. Don't be vulnerable to smart competitors who can steal many of your key 20%.

The sooner you identify your 20/80 customers, the sooner you'll profit from them.

Chapter 13
Lifetime value

What's a long-term customer worth to you?

LTV

Lifetime Value (LTV) ranks as marketing's most vital service trend. Foodstore genius Stew Leonard says "Every time I see a person leave with a frown, $50,000 just walked out the door." He knows LTV.

General Motors claims the LTV for a typical new customer entering a car dealership for the first time rings up to $400,000. The LTV of one food store customer chalks up $100,000 in just 20 years. One conservative formula says customer loyalty (LTV) returns 10 times the price of their first purchase.

The lights went on for me when I first found out how Cable TV companies are bought and sold. What do you pay to buy a Cable TV company? A few years ago, the going rate was $1,200 per household served. Meaning, my house is worth $1,200 value (double now) to a cable company.

Why? LTV of my payments. They can take it to the bank, literally.

Long-term evaluation

Efforts can't be judged against quarterly and yearly fiscal standards alone. LTV investment is for the long-term. It has a big payoff requiring a lot of commitment. Lifetime Value's customer focus brings with it a strong competitive edge against anyone not playing by its rules. Is any business that creates one-time customers efficient?. It's just "building sandcastles". A U.S. Government study confirmed that *it costs 5 times as much to gain a new customer as to keep an existing one.*

Create a customer, not a sale

The customer, too long ignored and exploited, now screams loud. Trend-setting smart marketers work for the long-term customer, not the quick sale…Whatever it takes to ensure their customer will return, and return, and return. LTV means building a relationship. It means dialog…listening to needs…caring, acting in the customer's interests and reaping long-term profit as a result.

Have you considered the LIFETIME VALUE of your customers?
What is the LTV of your best customers?

Chapter 14
Your value monopoly...niche

Answer. "Because less is more."
Question. "Why do I need a niche?

What is your niche? Niche is the thing that you do better than anyone else. Niche is what you specialize in...the specific thing that you offer which attracts and holds your best customers. **Your "VALUE MONOPOLY'.** Specialization. Superiority. Dominance. Differentiation.

Slice of the pie

Which slice of the pizza market would you like? Pizza's different players have carved out their own niches. Domino's set out to grab the home delivery market. Pizza Hut lays claim to the sit-down market. Little Caesar captured the take-out market with their 2 for 1 offer.

Since the vast majority of Pizza is ordered by phone, Canada's Pizza Pizza rings up sales with its "famous phone number" niche. Fully 80% of Torontonians can tell you Pizza Pizza's phone number 967 11-11. Pizza Pizza even puts the phone number in huge size on their store fronts. Other pizza companies may shoot for the lowest price slice. Every store must have a raison d'être, something unique.

Defending the territory

Niche requires the surrendering of other portions of the market in order to gain control of one specific aspect. **Less is more**. It's easier to defend a smaller territory because you can specialize and become exceedingly good at what you do.

Specialization

In specialization, you can buy in quantity in the specific attribute of your product and achieve economy of scale, i.e. the best price in what you do. Niche means knowing and giving your customers exactly what they need and want. Niche has struck heavy blows to traditional department stores. They are dinosaurs to a degree with even the name contradicting the principle of specialization.

Shades and varieties

Niches come in many varieties and shades; they can occupy portions of the price spectrum. Niche can come dressed in a "best service" suit, or best selection. If it's not "THE" something or other, it's not a niche. The best. The most. The cheapest... xxx-est.

I always chuckle at Garrison Keeler's Prairie Home Companion radio show on American Public Radio. One of his fictitious sponsors is "Ralph's Pretty Good Grocery Store". Ralph, it seems, has dug in his heels against the trend to niche. Ralph won't claim to be the best in anything. Perhaps his real niche is modesty.

One thing is sure. Businesses that ignore niche are about to do a dinosaur act and become extinct.

Take the niche test.

What do customers want that you do better than anyone else?

Are you telling people what you do best?

Chapter 15
Value In-your-face

All Business is Show Business!

Does business have to be boring? Wouldn't people rather do business with someone who makes life more fun, exciting, spicier?

Businesses who put pizzazz in their marketing shine brightly. Those who excel in putting fun in their promotion, win friends. Business people who have chutzpah stand out from the crowd and become high profile. They attract business.

An alive image, high awareness, center-stage visibility... powerful business assets these. They don't come from standing in a closet.

Stew Leonard operates a Connecticut food/dairy store that does $3,450 per square foot versus the industry average of about $300. What does he know that others don't? Stew has *Disney-like characters* circulating the store. On his parking lot you'll find *carved in stone*, his customer service policy. These are just two of the many show business finesses he pulls out of his hat.

Ray Kroc underpinned the growth of McDonalds on the show business foundation. Kids love Ronald McDonald. McDonalds refreshes the sale of their products with several layers of excitement and colorful promotion.

What show business specialties add to your customer experience?

"Show Business" can start with public speaking, trade shows, event marketing, networking, cross promotions with other businesses, loud and visible media presence…

Some of my clients do customer appreciation nights. Others do customer seminar evenings. They build in whatever excitement and luxuries they can afford to make it special for their customers.

What makes it show business?

What are the elements of show business? Think about it. What makes a Barnum and Bailey Circus? The sound of bands, the colorful dancing girls, the joy of performing clowns, bizarre performing elephants, the smell of popcorn, thrills, spills...

Pique the enjoyment for customers, employees, and owner; try a dash of "Show Business" in your business.

Can you list 20 ideas of "show business" things you might try?

Chapter 16
The 5 BASIC value tactics

When a sports team gets in a slump the coach says...
"We've got to get back to basics."

What are hockey's basics for instance? Shooting, Passing, Checking, Skating.

What are the basics tactics in the new value marketing game? As simply as they can be stated...

1. identify (identify and track individual customers on your computerized database)
2. satisfy (satisfy every time with your customer service system)
3. communicate (two way dialog to find customer needs and offer information)
4. reward (your loyalty plan to ensure they come back)

5. measure (what gets measured gets done. What gets measured gets improved)

Options or Necessary Actions?

These 5 basic tactics have ceased their optional role. I consider them absolutes in the new marketplace. Fading fast are the times when any business can successfully defend a dominant market position and omit any one of these 5 basics.

How well are you doing all 5 of these basic new value marketing tactics?

Chapter 17
Sitting on a goldmine?

DATABASE is for your profit.
Identify your customers!

Most Valuable Business Asset

What would you pay for your competitor's customer list? If someone offered your competitor your customer list, what would your competitor pay for it?

Isn't your greatest asset your collection of CUSTOMERS. Who are your customers? What do you know about them? How can you contact them?

You hold the database as the tangible form of that collection of customers. It stores their vital information, their accessibility, their transactions history, their interests. Choose whatever specific info you need to collect to help you increase business with them.

The Unknown Shopper

Gone are the days for product-oriented businesses. Retailers used to just sell merchandise and the customer was 'persona non grata'. The old business paradigm said "Buy low and sell high"…no thought for customer focus…no concern for service or building a relationship.

Someone should erect a monument to "the unknown customer". What abuse we all took under that old mentality. Stores didn't know who the customer was, or if they ever came back. Seldom did they really care.

Remember your customers

Never forget a customer.
Never let a customer forget you.

How? Database empowers you. **"We can now track 5 or 6 million customers for the same real cost as tracking a single customer in 1950".*
(Marketing Tools Magazine)

Your database retains who your customers are, and allows you to build a relationship with them.

Measure and target the best customers

Database shows who your best customers are. They are the 20% who account for 80% of your sales. Determine their Lifetime Value from the database. Know what they want so you can make them new specific offers. Keep track of how they respond. Your database measures results.

Work your database

When business gets slow, what do you do? WORK YOUR DATABASE. On rainy or snowy days you can go to your huge asset. Mail, fax, call or email to specific customers.

Customer retention

It still COSTS FIVE TIMES AS MUCH to gain a new customer as to keep an existing one. (U.S. Govt. survey) Search the database for customers who have become inactive. Ask them why and do something to get them back.

Segment the database

By finding out different interests and needs of your customers, you can sort from the list and make specific offers to sub-sets of the database. Above all, keep track of NEEDS. Your database becomes many different lists or databases. Each proves more workable and very profitable.

For restaurant clients, I suggest keeping track of birthdays and anniversaries. These are the two times of the year when customers are most likely to enjoy going to a restaurant. Consider these as profit opportunities. We contact the customer 10 days to 2 weeks in advance and make them a special offer.

Collect info from feedback cards

Much of the info we track comes from feedback cards. We ask the specific questions that gain the information that we can act on and profit from.

Are you fully activating a key business asset...your customer database?
Have you made your database a profit center?

63

Chapter 18
Value expectations

When prospects come to buy from a business, what expectations do they hold? What do they expect?

Do customers live in a vacuum? Or do they have some sort of performance standards in mind? Maybe even nebulous ones? Indeed they do.

Holiday Inn built on understanding expectations. They told us… "The best surprise is no surprise."

Every business must anticipate those expectations. How will customers score you against competitors? What areas will be important to them?

Don't fly blind. Find out.

Customers may spotlight perhaps 5 to 10 factors in your business. It varies. Ask your customer service people what your customers want when they come to you.

For example, when you order pizza delivery, how important is the TASTE? Do the TOPPINGS matter? How about the CRUST? Do you want the pizza delivered HOT?   Do you want it AS ORDERED or any old way it comes? Should the delivery be ON TIME or two hours late? What about VALUE, i.e. all these things factored against the price?

Once you identify the expectations, you need to rank them by importance.

Measure/track each expectation

When you offer comments cards, what do you put on the cards?   You list each of the expectations. Ask customers to score them by how they rate you...excellent, good, fair, could do better. Track each factor. If you happen to miss any important expectation, it will come out in the comments section. Probably your own customer service people will have a handle on them. You may rate well on 6 expectations and need improvement on another. Better you find out in your own survey, than lose customers and see the problem in your sales figures.

You'll know what to advertise. Won't these factors prove significant to prospects when you advertise?   Which one holds the most impact? How well do you compete in that critical factor?

If customers find a gap between their expectations and your level of performance, wont you lose?

A) Get a handle on the customer expectations.
B) Measure your performance through customer feedback.
C) Observe if there is a gap.
D) Use the gap as an opportunity to improve your competitiveness in that specific area.

What do your customers expect? What's most important to them in their purchase?

How well do you compete in each expectation?

Pizza *expectations*
Customer's Value Scorecard

1. **Taste**   Right spiciness, tomato flavor, tasty cheese and right consistency

2. **Toppings**   Selection of their favorite cheeses, right combination, right amount

3. **Crust**   Chewy, or crunchy to their judgment

4. **Hot**   on delivery. This factor is close-ended. Yes or No

5. **As Ordered**   If not, they're mad.

6. **Delivery**   in acceptable time. Tell them in advance if it's busy & you can't get it there.

7. **Price/ Value** for the money.
All the expectations factor in.

Chapter 19

Your customer service system

Do you want customers to enjoy great service some of the time, or every time?

To get customers back again and again (and reap the LTV, Lifetime Value) marketers must dedicate to serving customer needs and expectations. Not just lip service or wishing but a system that takes care of every single person. Should I be happy that the 9 people before me got great service and I didn't? Doesn't 90% good service sound OK? Not if I'm the 10% winding up on the short end.

Mapping your Moments of Truth

Does a customer service system cost you money or make you money? Jan Carlzon, President of SAS Airlines coined the term "moments of truth". These "MOT"s impress on customers a feeling about your service, whether good or bad. They can find your location easily; your parking is painless, your staff are friendly, trained and helpful from beginning to end. Have you walked through your customer's shoes? Have you experienced your service system steps the way they do? You need to map out your moments of truth to audit your system and its outcome. Make any adjustments or fine tuning. Too many businesses leave service to accident.

Building the system

For each point on the moments of truth, ask what would constitute 5 star service, 4 star, 3 star, 2 star, or 1 star. What level of service must we strive for? Then craft that level throughout the cycle of service. Record the process so it can be taught to each staff member.

Complaints

How do you handle complaints? Do your people know the system for taking care of customer complaints or do you kind of hope they will just go away? The Japanese call them "golden nuggets". A complaint is an opportunity to turn a customer's dissatisfaction around. Why not consider a complaint an opportunity to improve your system? Are your customer feedback cards prominently displayed to show that you value customer feedback? Do you follow up?

Recruiting

Disney has it right. Service starts with right recruiting. Disney doesn't try to make people nice; they hire nice people. People who care about customer needs!

Training

Isn't the best service training something you owe your employees? Don't you owe your customers the best training for your own people? Training is not an aspirin that you do once. Think of it as ongoing conditioning and refreshing.

Empowerment

Do all staff know your vision and mission? Can they list your business values so that they can make decisions the way you would make them? If so you can empower them. Customers want to deal with people who can make decisions.

Staff Reward

Do you reward your staff? They reflect you to the customer. Show them your appreciation. We will look at this vital action in a later chapter.

Mystery Shoppers
Do people like McDonald's assume that their people will carry out the system perfectly all the time? The top marketers keep tabs on their service system. They spot check it regularly and make improvements where weaknesses set in. Do you?

Customer Service Badge
If your service people were all wearing a badge to describe your customer services philosophy, what would it say?

The outcome feeling
The outcome of great service leaves a feeling. What feeling does your service leave?

Follow-up
How do you follow-up on a sale?

Feedback
Earlier we talked about customer feedback from the service system. Feedback completes the loop and leads to ongoing improvement.

Is your customer service a system, or just a hope and a prayer?
How do you guarantee service value?

Chapter 20
Communicating value

What Does Advertising Do? Depends on what you want and need it to do. I've heard people say..."Advertising doesn't work." But, what are their objectives?

Advertising will do the following things: (Which do you need?)

1. **AWARENESS**. It tells people you exist and builds a share of mind.

2. **POSTIONING**. It differentiates you by your major attribute/benefit.

3. **NEED**-identifier. e.g. McDonald's said "You deserve a break today." (the need? a break for folks all over America)

4. **TRUST**-builder. Your on-going presence reassures prospects. It makes a statement of your confidence in your business and what it

offers. Little advertising = little confidence; much advertising = much confidence. When you put your money where your mouth is, buying heavy advertising, it builds trust.

5. **IMAGE**. New or changed. You convey your business personality.

6. **LOYALTY**. You activate repeat customers. You remind people where you are and that you are their place to buy. You invite them to action. You build traffic.

7. **NEW CUSTOMERS**. Invite them in. Give them a reason. Inform them of your benefits. Stand out.

8. **DATABASE**-feeder. Identify who your customers are and track them. Run a prize draw where they can enter to win.

On your next campaign make sure you assess the importance to you of each of these factors. Does advertising work? Before anyone can judge, you have to determine what is the specific objective(s)? Then it's easier to determine how well the advertising worked.

Have you communicated your value? Advertising is how you do it.

Chapter 21
Positioning—differentiating value

Positioning forms your psychological packaging. That psychological package sets up your product or service to gain an advantageous value spot in the customer's mind.

Positioning's value roles

Differentiation

Just as products come in a box or package or carton, each product or service must be delivered in a psychological package. That packaging in the mind gives you meaningful differentiation from competitors. The differentiation comes with real or perceived customer benefits.

The American Express Card *-don't leave home without it.* Has AMEX not differentiated itself as the one with universal recognition! They present a powerful customer benefit by picturing people getting inconvenienced or stuck when they don't carry AMEX.

A strategy

Zeller's Discount Department Stores, for many years positioned with "where the lowest price is the law". That positioning liner also stated the corporate strategy so customers would know what to expect.

Lasting first impression

First impressions are lasting. So what lasting impression should your business leave? Positioning in fact delivers a promise pictured in that first impression. Make sure you live up to the promise. What was your first impression of "TOYS 'R' US'? It functions as both a name and a positioning statement. The playful, childlike creativity of the choice provided an instant comfort zone to kids and parents. Powerful.

Longevity

Correct positioning will often carry a company for decades. Longevity depends on:

* how clear you make the differentiation
* other changes in the marketplace
* memorability of the statement
* how heavily you implant the statement

77

Stay with positioning long term. It's expensive every time a company changes positioning. Long-term clear positioning is cost effective. What time frame has Prudential occupied "The Rock of Gibraltar" position?

A goodwill asset

Good positioning creates value. That value constitutes an asset. Consider it a front-line in the battle for dominant goodwill. For example... Xerox The Document Company. They create value for a simple photocopy by making it a "document". Xerox as a corporation has greater value with this positioning than it would without.

A headstart

In a 100-yard race would you like a 50 yard headstart? Superior positioning does just that. Competitors will be in a catch-up position.

A mission statement

When Avis said "We try harder" was it just a positioning statement? Employees got a message too.

An advertising foundation

Every advertisement carries the positioning statement. All advertising should state, enhance, reinforce and illustrate the company positioning. The Positioning platform supplies the foundation and the long-term content for the ad campaign.

A memory hook

The positioning statement gets you in the memory bank. "Campbell's Soup is MM'mm good."

A communication in headline form

When Canadian Tire needed to broaden the market's narrow perception of their stores they used a headline..."There's more to Canadian Tire than tires".

Tell what business you're in

When Lyn Bell Designs came to me, we shaped a positioning statement that clarified what business they were in:

LYN BELL of St. George
Fashions that say you're beautiful

The value of positioning
Good positioning = competitive advantage

Positioning powers up your business just as a rocket launcher boosts a satellite into orbit. It elevates your business into a desired niche in the customer's mind. Clear strong positioning can lift and keep you ahead of competitors. Wrong positioning leaves a business vulnerable.

Some types of positioning

TYPE	EXAMPLE
The name says it all	Toys 'R' Us Sports Experts
THE Category People *care specialists*	Green & Ross *The* car
Positioning Statements	Budweiser *The King of beers*
Differentiation	Burger King *have it your way*

Main attribute   Dominion Stores
It's mainly because of the meat

Broadening statement   Canadian Tire
There's more to Canadian Tire than tires

Slogan   Campbell's Soup,
MM'mm good

Category differentiation Zeller's *where the lowest price is the law*

The against position   7-UP *The uncola*

left brain/right brain   Hertz *puts you in the driver's seat*

Positioning tips
Use your positioning on everything.
Don't confuse it with another slogan.
Keep it short. Preferably in 3 words or less.
Examine it for aural suitability. That is...how does it sound?
Stay with it for the long-term.

Ideal positioning

What do you want from positioning?
Ideal positioning should communicate 4 things
(in three words or less):

1) Who you are
2) What you are
3) Where you are
4) How you're different

e.g. **KX 96**

Durham's new-country FM

Who they are...KX96. What they are...country music. Where they are... in Durham and at 96 on the FM dial. How they're different...they play new country.

What position do you own in the customer's mind now? What positions do your competitors own? What is your major attribute, niche, value monopoly? How can you best position yourself?

Chapter 22
NAME Value

Does the name Schweppes add value to the soft drink?

Some businesses make their name an asset. Others forever roll a stone uphill trying to overcome a non-performing name.

Usually one of the first actions when starting a business...select a name. This important activity generally gets all of about 75 seconds. Presto, there you have it. Once business cards are printed, the name is etched in stone. Never mind that we didn't put it up for scrutiny, or test it against attributes the customers want.

I ask you "How much would it cost you to change a poor name?" More importantly, "How much will it cost you if you don't change?"

Name benefit

A funny little episode recently illustrated the magic of the right name. A friend of mine was at a trade show demonstrating an Internet program where one can talk to people around the world. You simply connect a microphone to the computer and the program allows you to contact people who post their names on a chat board. My friend posted her name on the board. But there was very little response, which made it hard to do the demonstration. So my friend who is quite resourceful, changed her name on the list to "Bubbles". Amazingly... instant response.

What attribute would people be looking for in someone to chat with on the line? A sparkling personality! Exactly, and Bubbles tells it all in a name, probably more than any other name she could have chosen. It conjures up someone with an effervescent personality. She said it all in one word. In the name!

Think about the power of "Bubbles". Now think about your choice of business name. Does it attract business? Does it convey the main attribute of your product or service? Does it speak to the benefit of what you do? Does your name position you against your competition? Does it differentiate you, make you stand out, and place you ahead simply because you show in the name that you understand what the customer is thinking about?

David Ogilvy

Advertising guru David Ogilvy once suggested this idea.

List your benefits.

Survey to find which benefit customers rank first. Name the product/service after that benefit.

What's in a name? More than you'd think! How much effort is it worth?

As an asset, how does the value of your choice for a company name rate?

Should you change your name?
What will it cost if you don't?

— Spend whatever time it takes. The name lasts for a long time so get it right.

— Make sure you select from a wide choice. Limited selection offers limited opportunity to achieve greatness or creativity in your name choice.

— Test the name on a sample of the target group of customers. It's how they react that counts most.

85

Dennis O'Neill

Tips to choose THE best business Name

1. **Memorable** Pizza Pizza—967 11-11
    (80% of Torontonians know it by heart)
2. **Auditory** ("To utter a word, we first translate
    the letters into sound") How does it sound?
    e.g. Schweppes Gingerale
3. **Short** Toys 'R' Us   TOPS Supermarket
4. **Benefit**-connection to the product/service e.g.
    Sports Experts, Pampers, 7-11 (convenience
    stores), PROFIT Magazine
5. **Descriptive** of the product
    Timbits (Tim Hortons donut holes) Whopper,
    Big Mac, The Golf Doctor,
6. **Original**/unique Joe's Bar vs *Wild Thing*
7. **Legal** Availability   Don't use "R" Us
    It's contested by Toys "R" Us.
    McSleep (Motel) contested by McDonalds
8. **Product category** related. e.g. Burger King
9. **Avoid negative** connotations Chevy Nova In
    Spanish means "it doesn't run".
10. Ideally provides **differentiating** Positioning
    e.g. KX 96 Durham's New Country FM
    A-Who you are, B-What you are, C-Where
    you are, D-How you're different

11. **Non technical** not Smithville Mechanical Ltd. but Comfort Zone ... *The Heating/Cooling Specialists*
12. **Compatible** (image supportive) to goals, values, mission, vision

Chapter 23
Break-thru advertising

Clue #1. Is your advertising message breaking thru? John Wannamaker said .."*I know that half my advertising works; I just don't know which half.*"

The simple truth is, that doesn't have to be the case. In today's **"over-communicated society"**, the average North American gets bombarded by thousands of advertising messages a day. Estimates range as high as 5,000 per day. Your message must penetrate beyond all that noise and clutter.

Get your money's worth

How do you get your full dollar's worth every time you advertise?

Be certain you are communicating. How?

Here is the clear strategy to ensure your chances of getting thru.

1. Make it simple.

2. Say it often.

Look at McDonalds. It's what they have done for a long time.

They…1) make the message simple.
2) They say it often.

Make it simple.	Say it often.
Make it simple.	Say it often.
Make it simple.	Say it often.

Get cumulative power

The simple message sticks. Then when you run it again, it goes in deeper in the mind, then deeper and deeper. In the old days advertisers used price and item. Each ad started from zero. With Break-

89

thru power, you sharpen your simple message and run it each and every time. It builds on the memory of the last message. Every dollar spent, maximizes. Make it simple, say it often.

Sleep Country

Sleep Country Canada, and Sleep Country USA use the Break-thru technique. Their simple message... "Why buy a mattress anywhere else!" Every commercial runs the same line. They also try to put some urgency and excitement in each ad, a reason to buy now. But, everytime their goal is to impress the simple message... "Why buy a mattress anywhere else!"

What is your simple message?

This is the most important question you need to ask. Get it right.

The sooner you get your simple message, the sooner you'll get 100% back on your advertising investment.

Try to get your simple message in 3 words. If it takes 5 or 6, so be it. Shoot for 3. If you try for 5, you'll likely come out with 9 words. The more words, the more you undermine the simplicity.

So, what is your simple message?

_____ _____ _____

Chapter 24
Value remembered

"Memorability is the very soul of effective advertising psychology. If people don't remember your ad, the chances are they won't remember what you are trying to sell them."　　　(Chuck Blore)

Value in being remembered

Your value depends directly on your ability to have people remember you, your business, your differentiation, your benefits.

How can you get people to remember you and your message?

'The 3 laws of memory'

At college, I learned about "The 3 laws of memory" as they called them. Initial impact, Repetition, Association. I felt grateful then to identify those three.

Having worked in a field where memorability hugely matters, experience has taught me some new tricks. Here is my list:

The tools of memorability
1. initial impact
2. repetition
3. association
4. musical context (jingles, lyrics)
5. emotional context
6. rhyme/cadence
7. brevity (think short)
8. simplicity
9. exaggeration/distortion
10. paint a picture
11. story flow/context
12. alliteration
13. write it down/file it
14. mnemonics (1st letters spell a word)
15. dramatization
16. gesturing (I saw this in an article recently)

_____

_____

Can you add to the list?

You can utilize the list of memorability techniques. They empower your communication! What's the point in communicating if the point is not remembered.

The human memory astounds me. Can the human mind recall up to 50,000, perhaps 100,000 songs? I believe so. Who knows the actual number? Bob Hopes' capacity for jokes astounds me. His repertoire numbers hundreds of thousands of jokes.

The mind works by ear.

Believe it or not. Most of the tools in the memorability kit are aural in nature.

In their book *POSITIONING; The Battle For Your Mind*, Al Ries & Jack Trout make some startling statements:

*"Try to memorize a poem without reading it out loud. It's far easier to memorize written material if we reinforce **the aural component, the working language of the brain**."*

"When words are read, they are not understood until the visual/verbal translator in your brain

takes over to make aural sense out of what you have seen."

"Did you think Hubert and Elmer were bad names? If so you must have translated the printed words into aural equivalents. Because Hubert and Elmer don't look bad. They only sound bad."

A friend of mine has a marvelous memory. One day, he said, "Do you remember such and such a meeting?" I did. (It took place decades before) He said "Do you remember what so-and-so said". I said I hadn't a clue. Then I watched and heard him prompt his memory. He closed his eyes, and said... "Da Daa Da Daa, Da Daa Daa Daa etc." He was recalling the cadence. Once he had the cadence, it recalled the exact words, even after 30 years. I marveled. I had just observed him use one of his many techniques that made his recall superior to most people. Yet his methods are teachable he insists.

Do you always examine a message whether you say it or write it? Do you check it for its aural quality? That's what gets through to the brain, to the memory.

Stick that in your ear.

Chapter 25
Value repeated…frequency

One more time! Don't say it once. Say it again. Say it often. Frequency. Frequency sells. Tell 'em again.

If you tell people enough times, eventually they'll get it. They'll do it. Frequency is a factor of memory, and it wears through big time as a convincer. Like water dripping on a rock.

Forgetting

The Ebbinghaus curve of forgetting shows that in 20 minutes people forget 42% of what they have just learned. After nine hours they have forgotten 64%. With each passing day memory grows dimmer.

So, what to do about it?
Say it again. Say it often. Say it often. Frequency.

Learning

Think back to school. When test time came, we went over the points again and again, till we had them in mind. No different in the marketplace. Say it again. Say it often.

The psychology is simple. People have to go through **3 stages**

* <u>curiosity</u>   1)What is it?
* <u>recognition</u>   2)(I've noted it before) What of it?
*<u>decision</u>   3)What am I going to do about it?

source— Prof. Herbert Krugman

Even when people decide they might do something, it may not be until the time is right. So the frequent reminder functions as:

** **the engine of psychological progression** and
** **the memory sustainer till the opportune time to act.**

Say it often.
Don't stop saying it.
Say it again. Frequency wins.
Play it again Sam.

Chapter 26
Value loyalty

Isn't loyalty a two-way street? What's your reward system for building loyalty with your customers? You have to earn loyalty. How? Do you have a loyalty plan? It's not an option any more...it's now a BASIC in today's marketing.

So how does your system work?

You want clients to do something for you...i.e. be loyal. How do you show loyalty to them and add to the relationship?

Hats off to Canadian Tire, long a top loyalty plan contender with their Canadian Tire money. You can't spend it at Wal-Mart but have to return to Canadian Tire. That's the idea. When you go back, they give you more Canadian Tire money and on and on.

Loyalty plans come in assorted styles, shapes and varieties.

Look at Zeller's Club Zed.(Now H.B. Rewards) Each purchase gains points on your Club Z card. You redeem points for merchandise. Customers think twice about spending somewhere else knowing that they are earning points towards some desired reward.

Frequent flyer clubs

The airlines learned early on to use unsold inventory to reward customers for spending a higher share of their travel dollars. They take something of no value, unused inventory, and make it into a valuable reward.

Air Miles takes the airlines seat inventory (often unsold) and uses it as a loyalty reward for various other businesses and services. A win/win/win. The airlines create demand for inventory and profit by it. The individual participating businesses increase share and the customer is rewarded for loyalty.

How about the donut store that gives customers a loyalty card. You buy 9 cups of coffee and they reward you with the 10th one free. Tim Horton has taken it a step further with their "role up the rim to win contest". The more you buy the greater your chances of winning a prize. And they put a little fun into the act because you can win right on the spot.

The varieties of loyalty plan are unlimited. Still, many businesses find it difficult to construct a suitable loyalty plan.

Client seminars

I suggested the necessity of a loyalty plan to one client of mine, a computer networking solutions operation. The owner said "We don't have one; what could we possibly do?" I suggested "What about seminars for your best customers." He said "We don't really have anyone to do seminars." I said "Why not get your suppliers to provide the expertise which they more than willingly did." Not only that... the suppliers already happened to have expensive, polished video presentations to support their accomplished presenters.

My client now does two seminars a year with increasingly large turn-outs as word spreads. The client-appreciation hospitality builds a bond with customers. Customers also are impressed to see the strong relationship my client has with his international suppliers, which is an added value to each of them as end-customers. The night is 1) fun, 2) educational/informative, 3) confidence - building, 4) an opportunity for dialog between customer and business. That dialog turns into the customer discussing further problems and needs. Every problem and need is an opportunity to offer a solution which leads to more business and a further growth of the relationship.

Say thanks over lunch

Your loyalty plan may be as simple as taking your top 10, 20, or 50 clients to lunch.

Client appreciation night

I know a printing company which won the award for entrepreneur of the year in their area. They host an annual customer appreciation night. They have fabulous buffet dinner, open bar, several bands, and just a wonderful night of hospitality to say thank you to all their customers.

Maybe you choose to send a very special thank you note.

Thanksgiving

I have several loyalty plans; one is simply a Thanksgiving card expressing my appreciation for being able to work with a person and their business. Thanksgiving cards are big in the U.S. but almost unknown in Canada. In most cases I'm the only one sending a Thanksgiving card so my message stands alone for maximum impact.

Birthday cards

Several of my clients, particularly restaurants, sends birthday cards. The card of course presents an offer to come out for their birthday dinner and receive a special free dessert.

You can devise a unique and appropriate loyalty plan for your business. Spend a little thought and creativity. Loyalty plans pay dividends so take the time and effort to show customers that you are prepared to do your part to earn their loyalty.

How does your loyalty plan work?

Chapter 27
Appreciating valued employees

"Thank you, I really **appreciate** that!"

Everyone's greatest human need is to be *appreciated.* Appreciation builds loyalty. People crave recognition or feedback on results.

Any feedback people want must start with appreciation of what they are doing well.

(Appreciation helps earn the right to suggest ways for them to get even better.) How much do you show appreciation to your associates?

How can we offer appreciation?

1. deserved compliments
2. thank you's
3. encouragement
4. timely applause
5. awards
6. right to pride of achievement
7. trust

8. empowerment
9. opportunity for promotion
10. feeling of belonging communicated
11. feeling of being needed communicated
12. input in decision-making
13. being kept informed
14. attention
15. documentation of achievement
16. additional training (investment in them)
17. salary increases on merit
18. profit sharing
19. commissions
20. bonus
21. time off as a reward
22. perks...tickets, trips etc.

Can you add to the list?

Many of the above cost zero dollars. Shouldn't appreciation be served up generously when warranted!

Wouldn't you rather work for, or own **a business that is *appreciating*?**

Chapter 28
Measuring value throughout your business.

How does your business measure up?

What gets measured gets improved, said the Sage. What ought you to measure?

What gets measured gets done. Does measurement sometimes give the prod we need? Measurement helps defeat sloth.

Measurement documents personal productivity. A friend asked "How was your week?" Before I could respond he said "How would you know?" How do we measure if we had a good week? Learning to measure challenges us.

Good measurements bring security. Is your business growing? How do you know? Perhaps your business is increasing 4 or 5 % a year while your competitors are averaging 9 or 10%? Even with sales going up, your market share is shrinking?   Are you measuring market share? Does measuring just sales suffice?

Measurement allows tracking. Does your customer service match competitors? Is your customer service improving, holding, or even declining? How would you know? Should you be measuring it? Are you thinking about how?

Measurement allows you to build a success formula. Ever see a great chef work? They work from a recipe carefully following the measurement for each ingredient.

Measurement ensures focus, and clarity. How do you measure your advertising? Do you just spend and hope? Can you prove that you got your moneys worth? Can you document what worked and what didn't?

Measurement allows comparison. Have you ever put together a competitive analysis to compare your business with your main competitors in each and every aspect? We're not talking measurement paralysis but how do you know what needs fixing or improving? Who are the models of excellence in each aspect of your business. How do you measure up in each component.

People generally agree that measurement makes sense. Many just don't know what specifically to measure. Some operate from a seriously impoverished model when it comes to measurement. *Not knowing what and how to measure* quite often prompts people to call me, "The business growth coach".

How serious are you about your business growth? Growth demands measuring the process all along the way, long before the final sales figures. By the time of the final sales results, it may be too late.

> ***What should you be measuring?***
> ***When will you start?***
> ***What do you measure?***
> ***What can be measured?***
> ***What should you measure?***

The challenge

Most people find a huge challenge in trying to find what to measure. We have impoverished models.   We seldom exercise our minds in devising measurement tools.

Look to your automobile

Consider your car.   What do you measure there?   Speed.   Mileage driven.   Gas gauge. Battery charge.   Clock.   Engine temperature.   A whole range of essentials.   Now apply that scope to your business.

Your INDEX of Measurement Tools
Measurement tools come in many shapes and sizes

Try expanding your thought horizons with these words: What measurement comes to mind from each of these words?

gauge	benchmark	track
calculate	enumerate	quantify
compute	grade	scope
rate	relate	compare
graduate	equate	level
weigh	match	balance
appraise	assess	reckon
survey	index	grid
arrange	classify	sort

scale	divide	subdivide
prioritize	collect	list
record	fit	tabulate
magnify	spread	estimate
rank	describe	count
mark	demarcate	increment
average	mean	portion
evaluate	deduce	take the pulse
pinpoint	identify	scrutinize
isolate		

Now find the right scales to *assess your success*.

Is there a better way for you to measure?

Improvement

Remember…**what gets measured gets improved.**
Which areas do you want to improve?

Chapter 29
Maintaining personal value

Stop! Don't become obsolete.

How would you feel about a medical doctor who just sees patients? Doesn't read. Doesn't study new advances in the field. Is that OK? Do you just accept their personal devaluation?

Should customers patronize business people who fail to learn, grow, improve?

Have you asked yourself "How am I improving myself personally? What steps am I taking to self improvement?" In the fast changing marketplace, each of us can now expect to have 5 careers. Are we shedding the old paradigms? *Worth repeating is* Charles Exley, CEO, NCR Corp.*"I've been in this business 36 years. I've learned a lot—and most of it doesn't apply anymore."*

Try listing the things you are doing to keep up. If the list looks insignificant and short, let this article be your wake-up call.

Personal value maintenance steps

1. How about a **reading program**. Formalize your reading for specific needs.
2. Have you sought a **mentor**? Find a person who can lift you to new heights in a chosen field. That person may enjoy helping people and offer you much.
3. **Audio tape** learning programs use time wisely, perhaps when you're driving.
4. Enroll in a **formal course** or several courses.
5. **Networking** for contacts and sources offers big pay-offs.
6. Use the **Internet** to search. Research. Learn. Study.
7. Do you set out a **written plan with specific goals** and actions.
8. Measure your actions, programs and progress and successes in specific areas.
9. Do you **try new things**?

10.Master skills and routines through **practice**. Sales people should role-play. What do you practice. Athletes do it in sports, every day.

…What else might you do to increase your personal value?

Lots of people feel confident in their education degree. Think about this. "Half the skills of technical workers become obsolete within three to seven years of completing a formal education."
Source-the Canadian Labor Market and Productivity Centre

Obsolescence comes by default. Why let it? If you grow yourself continually, your business value grows with you.

Would someone accuse you of being obsolete?

How do you keep up?

Chapter 30
The value of your time

What could possibly be more valuable than our time? Life consists of two things…time and energy. I always appreciate people who truly serve community causes in an unselfish way. They give their time and their energy. In reality they sacrifice a small piece of their life for others. How scarce a commodity is our time!

Why do some people accomplish more in a day than others?

Why do you get more done some days than other days?

How can we accomplish more in any given time?

How can we get the most from our time?

Priorities

Doesn't best use of time boil down to priorities? What priorities have you set for your time?

Earlier chapters already covered some of the most critical factors in shaping time value.

Vision… to know where we are going.

Written goals…to provide specific objectives.

A business MAP…brief plan to show us the way.

Mission statement…to focus all our actions.

Values…identify what's most important to us.

Time management

Time management companies abound. They provide invaluable service to so many people. Imagine if you only increase your own time efficiency by 5%? What value does that return?

I love Peter Drucker's words *"Until you can manage your time, you can manage nothing else."*

Time focus

"Your life will flow toward where you spend your time." How do you actually spend your time? Have you charted your time for a week to find out? It's your life.

Identify time wasters

What enemies steal your time? Have you targeted your personal time enemies? Why not zero in on the ones that rob you? Those time thieves prevent us from so many more gains and wins which we should capture and enjoy.

Business time wasters:

lack of priorities
personal disorganization
lack of self-discipline
crisis management
attempting too much (from lack of planning)
drop-in visitors (no specific purpose for visit)
ineffective delegation
procrastination
the inability to say NO

Some people add telephone interruptions to the list. I want telephone calls but I understand why someone would put it on the list.

When you have say 20 items to do in a day, are they all equally vital? Can you group them into A-importance, B-importance and C-importance? Get the A's done. Too often we spend too much time on the C's. You can go with a more complex system if you choose. The more direct we act in time use, the more our success expands. Some folks engage in things that look busy; sadly, they get very little done.

Working smarter

Focus on Main Action Priorities…(your MAP's). The Map's move you toward the key goals. Working harder may often prove counter productive. The activity falls short of prime needs. Working smarter requires right direction, not just bluster.

There's a time for everything

Often we become tired. "Fatigue makes cowards of us all" said famous NFL coach Vince

Lombardi. At that time our body says 'rest'. Take a break. Do something else. Look for balance.

Timing

Some people achieve more in the morning. Others do better at night. It makes basic sense to work when you can produce the most.

Down time

I've never felt too happy about sickness. My value to myself, or to anyone, approaches zero when I get sick. Personal value increases directly with radiant health. What health strategy do you carry out? Do you have a plan to preserve your health?

Longevity

Most of us would like to live a long happy life. We want more time. We desire quality time. Good health offers our best hope of longevity. Look to the 2,000's. Man may soon increase his life span to 100, some say perhaps 200 years. Few of us look forward to when time runs out.

What's the value of time?
Do you value your time?
What is your time worth?
Do you get the most from your time?
What actions do you do in your space of time?
How can you improve your time use?

Chapter 31
WINNING

Every win adds value

Every win you enjoy makes a deposit in your bank of success. Every success increases your experience. Every success you enjoy adds stature. Stature increases your value.

Each win should build your confidence. A more confident person achieves more. So the snowballing effect of increased value feeds your whole value-building machine.

Human problems

Too bad most people suffer from compound diseases!

    1) short memory

    2) excess humility

We have daily wins and successes. So soon we forget. Most people (not everyone) will say..."Ah shucks, it really wasn't much". But it really was.

A friend of mine suggested that I keep score of my wins. Each day in my pocket calendar, he proposed that I write down my wins of the day. He suggested I asterisk the big ones. This way I couldn't forget those wins.

That worked well. Still the wins don't exhibit their power unless they all show together on the same page. So I came up with the WIN SCORECARD idea.

The Win Scorecard

"Confidence is the memory of success". By writing down the many success events we complete, we defeat the bad memory factor.

As you score a win in some way which you feel worthy, you list what it was and the date on one line on the scorecard. At first you may have a win every day or two. Soon you find you can win fairly often.

Then it occurs to you..."maybe I can score a win every day. Maybe I can hit two home-runs today in business". Somehow, it starts to happen. Perhaps it happens much like the baseball hitter whose batting average is say 239. But with runners in scoring position, he hits 390. Why? Does he bat better because he psyches himself up more with runners on base? Perhaps the psyching up factor kicks in on your Win Scorecard project.

Funny, but you will probably find yourself scoring a win every day. You come to believe you can. And you can when you believe.

Your personal inventory

What value do you have as a person? as a business person?

Have you ever completed a personal inventory? Your inventory of achievements in large part determines your value as a person. Your inventory includes major character traits, various experiences, proven skills and accomplishments.

When you document all those factors with evidence of each, you prove your value. Don't think of it as a resume which usually focuses on employment history. Your personal inventory spotlights your achievements. It highlights your true value.

The personal inventory cures 'false humility' from which most people suffer.

You may be surprised at your true value.

Try writing yourself a letter covering all your personal inventory. Quote people who said you have a certain quality. Refer to documents and your acomplishments. You will find that you are a much more valuable person than you have previously allowed yourself to believe.

When will you draw up your personal inventory?

Wouldn't you profit from keeping a Win Scorecard?

Your Win Scoreboard

Confidence is *the memory of success.*

WINS are examples of my success, evidences of my working smarter, not just harder. Being alert to my successes & documenting them, will cause me to believe in myself. That confidence then helps me be even more successful and more valuable.

MEASURING SUCCESS=Counting my WINS

Wins	Date

Dennis O'Neill

_____

_____

_____

_____

_____

_____

_____

_____

_____

_____

_____

_____

_____

_____

_____

_____

— (page 1 of 500+)

Chapter 32
Value payoffs

The benefits test. What is a Benefit?

Have you identified, polished and communicated your value to the customer? Customers rate your value against the benefits you state or demonstrate.

I prefer to employ the word **PAYOFFS** rather than benefits. Customers make their decision based on their own values which are the inner needs. Often the benefits are used to rationalize their decision.

What are payoffs or benefits?

Benefits are "well done's"...something that does well in satisfying a need.

The word benefit means NEED SATISFIERS.

Be sure the customer will ask "What's in it for me?" (**WIIFM**) Your benefits must answer.

Focus on the big question ...

What need does your product or service serve?

Polish your payoffs

You will realize a huge payoff yourself by spending time clarifying your benefits. List them. Prioritize them. Polish them. Plus them. Do they suffice? Do you need more payoffs to fulfill client needs?

How do you identify a benefit?

Try this exercise. Start by asking... does it satisfy the need in providing any of the following:

gain	competitive edge	advantage
profit	win/win	something special

plus	bonus	extra
usefulness	worth	merit
prize	differentiation	discovery
effective	solutions	power
conducive to…	efficient	new
improvement	economy	help
support	lead(leadership)	value added
easy..ease	opportunity	answers
strength	winner	avoidance
nullify	growth	security
leading edge	safety	etc…

(Build your own list)

Consider values towards (wants), and values away (avoidance's).

What does the buyer want most, or want to avoid most?

Have you listed your benefits and prioritized them?

Select the most important.

Then spend time polishing the best wording to communicate the benefit/payoff.

Chapter 33
Selling value

Hats off to the sales professional!

"Sales people count the most. They're the highest form of life. If they succeed, we all eat. Everything flows from the successful sale."

---

quote from Jerry White,
(business & financial guru)

Sales and selling have been maligned, often for good cause. Unfortunately lots of people don't conduct the selling process professionally. True selling by professional sales people looks for a win/win. They find a need and fill the need with the best solution. What a noble career...helping people solve their problems. What more 'Christian' endeavor could a person in business do!

What salespeople do

In an earlier chapter we looked at the value definition.

$$\text{Value} \quad = \quad \frac{\text{Need } + \text{ Trust}}{\text{price}}$$

We found that the reason people don't buy boils down to ...they don't see the value. So, when they do buy they grasp the value. What then does the sales person do in selling?

They help the customer to assess the value. Value needs to be identified, demonstrated, illustrated, proved and delivered. Sometimes value needs to be created, or added to. The professional sales person deals in value. He or she establishes value. The customer may then elect to buy with confidence.

Establishing value

Establishing value requires two major components.

1) The customer must see or be shown the need. If I have no need, there is no value. Sometimes prospects can be shown that the need exceeds what they had presumed. That larger need translates to greater value which becomes a higher incentive to buy. The sales person's function is to explore and expand the need to its maximum.

2) Even when a customer perceives the need, they must trust the seller or the producer of the good or service. The more trust, the more value. The less trust, the less value. If the buyer can't depend on the seller or manufacturer to deliver as promised in filling the need, the product/service surely devalues.

Needs analysis and probing the need

Needs analysis requires a person who excels in the art of questioning. Questions open the mind. Questions bring out client problems. For selling Sales people need to make themselves an expert questioner. Try writing out your 5 best questions before any sales call. Polish them. Consider the sequence. See how much power your questions will offer.

Maximizing the sale

I made a call on a prospect, the CEO of a firm.

<u>stage one</u>

I asked a series of probing questions. The CEO revealed a need and I proposed a solution. He said "wonderful". There I had a sure sale for X dollars. I would have been satisfied in times past, before I knew the value formula. But we know the value formula… value = $\frac{\underline{need + trust}}{price}$

<u>stage two</u>

So I said "Now that we have a solution, would it make sense to bring in your General Manager to make sure he is on-side?" The CEO said, "Good idea". When we explained the concept to the GM, he said "That's great, but what we really need is (such and such)". I proposed a solution. They both thought it would work well and now I had a sale for X+Y dollars.

<u>stage three</u>

Again, we know the value formula so I kept pushing to find the full need. Thus I said "in order for this plan to work, wouldn't it make sense to have the sales department on-side?" They agreed. They brought in the sales manager, a bright young lady. When she heard the plan, she said "that's OK but what we really need is (such and such)". I asked if I could think about the need for a week and return.

They agreed.

<u>stage four</u>

I returned with a proposed plan and all three loved it. Now I had a sale for X+Y+Z dollars. We know the formula and the greater the need, the greater the value. Now I suggested that to make certain the plan worked, wouldn't it make sense to have the individual sales people informed. I told them I'd be happy to come in on my time and explain the deal at one of their sales meetings. They quickly agreed. Guess what? The sales people said... "all of those things are fine but what we really need in the field is such and such". I proposed a solution. Everyone agreed. Now my sale was for X+Y+Z+K dollars.

The CEO did not even question my price. He called his secretary and instructed her to write check requisitions for the dates I had proposed.

As the need expanded, the customer value went up. In tandem, so did the amount of my sale.

At that moment events proved that selling gets rewarded directly with the size of the need. More need, more value.

The other factor of selling, trust, revealed itself here. That organization had a need we never really talked about. Poor inside communication. All memos came from the top. Lower levels didn't get a chance to inform higher levels of their needs.

My needs-probing helped them and built trust for me as I stayed with them through each step.

How do you build trust.

To start you need rapport. Often trust is enhanced by a third party endorsement or a common friend. Trust builds on strong follow-through and delivery on promises. Many factors can build trust. How do you build trust with prospects? That trust pays back. It boosts your value. What else could you do to increase your value?

Need versus market

Yes there may be a need.
But, is there a market?

An educational book publishing company had many teachers telling them of the need for books on certain subjects.

Several times the publishers produced such books only to find that none of the school boards were in the market for them.

There was a need, but there was not a market.

The words
NEED and MARKET
are **not** interchangeable.

Chapter 34
Value pricing

What price should your product/service charge?

A sales focus mired in price-cutting means hell to pay!

One of the biggest market diseases has emerged as cut rate pricing. Let's bite the bullet. Can't we stop kidding ourselves about giving the product away. Afraid to lose the sale, sales departments often cave-in on price. Usually the justification is "We got the sale didn't we?

Non-professional or untrained sales people and marketers resort to price cutting when they don't understand value. Value does not usually mean lowest price. It considers the value formula...$value = \dfrac{need + trust}{price}$

The price is driven by what's above the line; how much need and how much trust.

That is …price gets set by how much customers need the product or service with its unique features and benefits as well as how much trust-equity the seller commands.

Under-pricing pitfalls

Seldom will businesses fail from over-pricing. They fail because their prices can't cover costs. Did we really want that low price sale? Was it a victory or a defeat? How did that sale affect the bottom line? Do we really want every customer's business? Really?

Truth is…there are two kinds of customers. Profitable and unprofitable. The secret… lose the unprofitable accounts to the competition. Let that type of client infect competitors but not you.

What really happens when you continually grab clients by price-cutting? Habitual price-cutting erodes our systems. The needed margin escapes. The price-cutting disease in time costs us our good people, our facilities, our better systems, the advantages that gave us competitive edge. In short time we can't afford to deliver our previous competitive advantage. At that point one gets sucked into the quagmire of more and more price-cutting.

One client first contacted me with just such a scenario. I requested a brochure from him and each of his top 10 competitors. There were none. Their sales departments lacked any other value dimensions to sell. So it fell to price.

What is the antidote to price-cutting? For my client, two courses of action had to be taken. One, find the basis of value that made his product superior. Two, communicate that value first to the sales department and then to the customer.

Commoditization

We must understand this...*"There is no such thing as a commodity. All goods and services are differentiable."* (Theodore Levitt)

I express it this way to the sales department... **"All 'widgets' are not equal."** It must be the first factor out of the salesperson's mouth. "All widgets are not equal". They have to believe this statement and they must prove it to the customer. If all widgets were equal, then price would be the only basis on which to buy them.

All widgets are not equal. Your brochure, your advertising, your sales materials, your sales people...everything you do must state and prove "all widgets are not equal". You must show how you are unique, different, better. Something the prospect needs. That difference justifies the price. Sales training must include the way you prove your product/service superiority. Remember, all widgets are not equal.

If you get into price-cutting, pretty soon you can't afford to continue producing whatever makes your product better.

Price-cutting reflects terrible marketing. It fails to establish a value advantage. Price-cutting identifies lazy, gutless, ignorant, unprofessional selling.

"Mr. or Ms Customer...do you think all widgets are equal". This widget does much more than other widgets. This widget does things you've said you clearly want and need. So wouldn't you expect it to cost slightly more? It does, because it delivers the best value.

Do we have the courage to say..."They sell price; we sell value."

Chapter 35
The value of implementation

Get it done! Value depends on completion. "I know what to do... I just can't seem to get it done." Hear those words of the business person who often fails at 'getting round to it'.

Can't seem to *Get around to it*
How often do you say these same words? I just can't seem to get around to it. Great plan! Useless if it never happens.

Implementers
"Blessed are the implementers for they get things done". Implementers are motivated by the question...WHEN? When will we get at this? When will we get this done? Time motivates the implementer. They can't get at it soon enough...a "bias for action". General George Patton said

"A good plan violently executed now is better than a perfect plan next week."

When Implementers always have the "when" question at the top of their mind. When can we get at this? When can we get this done?

****

<u>The 3 laws of action</u>

1) JUST DO IT!
2) READY, <u>FIRE</u>, AIM
3) WHAT IS IN MOTION, STAYS IN MOTION (i.e. MOMENTUM)

****

What's the value of a half finished painting? What's the value of a house that sits a couple years with no roof?

Too often we dilly dally in analysis paralysis. Call on your daily motivation question... WHAT WILL I IMPLEMENT TODAY? Tomorrow may be too late. Do it NOW. Winning starts with beginning.

It has no value until it exists!

—TAKE ACTION—